Green Homes

by Saranne Taylor

Illustrated by Moreno Chiacchiera and Michelle Todd

Crabtree Publishing Company

Crabtree Publishing Company
www.crabtreebooks.com
1-800-387-7650

Published in Canada
616 Welland Ave.
St. Catharines, ON
L2M 5V6

Published in the United States
PMB 59051, 350 Fifth Ave.
59th Floor,
New York, NY

Published in 2015 by CRABTREE PUBLISHING COMPANY.

Author: Saranne Taylor
Illustrators: Moreno Chiacchiera, Michelle Todd
Project coordinator: Kelly McNiven
Editor: Shirley Duke
Proofreader: Crystal Sikkens
Production coordinator and prepress technician: Ken Wright
Print coordinator: Katherine Berti

Photographs:
Pg 4 – Featherstone Young
Pg 10 – (t) luckypic (bl) Jennifer_Loring@Flickr (br) Ragne Kabanova
Pg 11 – (t) Victorgrigas / Wikipedia (bl) Africa Studio (br) Berents
Pg 12 – Tupungato
Pg 13 - Eugene Sergeev
Pg 15 - Andrewglaser / Wikipedia
Pg 21 – (tl) Sealstep (tr) Tom Harpel / Wikipedia (bl) meanep (br) Winning7799
Pg 22 – (l) Dr Ajay Kumar Singh (r) Tutti Frutti
Pg 23 - (bl) photoBeard (br) Gerry Thomasen / Wikipedia
Pg 25 – (main) Colin Rose / Wikipedia (inset) Bildagentur Zoonar GmbH
Pg 27 – (main) Heather Nicaise (inset) Happy Little Nomad / Wikipedia

All images are Shutterstock.com unless otherwise stated.

Every attempt has been made to clear copyright. Should there be any inadvertent omissions, please notify the publisher.

Printed in Hong Kong/082014/BK20140613

Library and Archives Canada Cataloguing in Publication

Taylor, Saranne, author
Green homes / Saranne Taylor ; illustrated by Moreno Chiacchiera and Michelle Todd.

(Young architect)
Includes index.
Issued in print and electronic formats.
ISBN 978-0-7787-1452-1 (bound).--ISBN 978-0-7787-1456-9 (pbk.).--
ISBN 978-1-4271-1579-9 (pdf).--ISBN 978-1-4271-1575-1 (html)

1. Ecological houses--Juvenile literature. I. Chiacchiera, Moreno, illustrator II. Todd, Michelle, 1978-, illustrator III. Title.

TH4860.T39 2014 j728'.047 C2014-903592-6
C2014-903593-4

Library of Congress Cataloging-in-Publication Data

Taylor, Saranne, author.
Green homes / by Saranne Taylor ; illustrated by Moreno Chiacchiera and Michelle Todd.
pages cm. -- (Young architect)
Includes index.
ISBN 978-0-7787-1452-1 (reinforced library binding) -- ISBN 978-0-7787-1456-9 (pbk.) --
ISBN 978-1-4271-1579-9 (electronic pdf) -- ISBN 978-1-4271-1575-1 (electronic html)
1. Sustainable buildings--Juvenile literature. 2. Sustainable architecture--Juvenile literature. 3. Architecture, Domestic--Juvenile literature. 4. Dwellings--Juvenile literature. I. Chiacchiera, Moreno, illustrator. II. Todd, Michelle, 1978- illustrator. III. Title. IV. Series: Young architect.
TH880.T385 2015
720.47--dc23
2014020113

Contents

Introduction

Living in a green home doesn't mean your house is painted green! It means that it's been built with materials which are safe for our planet. Today, more and more people want to protect Earth's environment. They want houses that are specially designed to be environmentally friendly and that make use of natural materials.

The great thing about being an architect is that you can create your own designs. So let's find out about all the great ways you can become a green architect!

Orchid House is an architect's design for an eco-home in England.

Orchid House at night

Eco-designs

Green homes are also called eco-homes. Eco is short for ecology, which is the study of how living things live in their environment.

Eco, or green, homes can come in all shapes and sizes and architects use a lot of imagination coming up with designs. But most important, these homes are environmentally friendly. They use materials that are safe for our planet or are made from natural products.

Orchid House is one example of an eco-house. It has wood tiles on the outside that allow it to blend in with the forest around it. It is designed with a special heating system which uses warm water from natural sources underground. It also faces the Sun, which provides extra heat in the winter!

Create an earthship

An earthship is a type of eco-home that is built and powered by its environment and recycled materials.

One side of the earthship is almost all windows while the other side is built tightly into the side of a hill.

There are **solar panels** and a **wind turbine** on the roof.

Water tanks at the back of the house collect rainwater.

The outside, or **external**, walls are thick. The inside, or **internal**, walls are often made from recycled materials.

Other materials used to build an earthship are made of materials found in the local area.

Plants are grown inside and outside the building all year round, making part of this home really green!

wind turbine
hillside
solar panels
window
recycled tires
plants
water tank
septic tank

Architect's notebook

Design features

solar power

The windows face south to get the most Sun. The Sun's power lights and heats the living space. This kind of natural heating is called passive solar power.

hillside

To make sure the earthship stays warm, the north walls are built into the hillside to protect them in cold weather.

tires

The walls are often built using recycled materials, such as old tires. The thick walls help keep the inside of the building at the same temperature, so in the summer the house is cool and in winter it is warm.

On the roof, solar panels soak up the sunlight. They change, or convert, the energy from the Sun into electricity. They do this by using specially treated plates called **photovoltaic cells**.

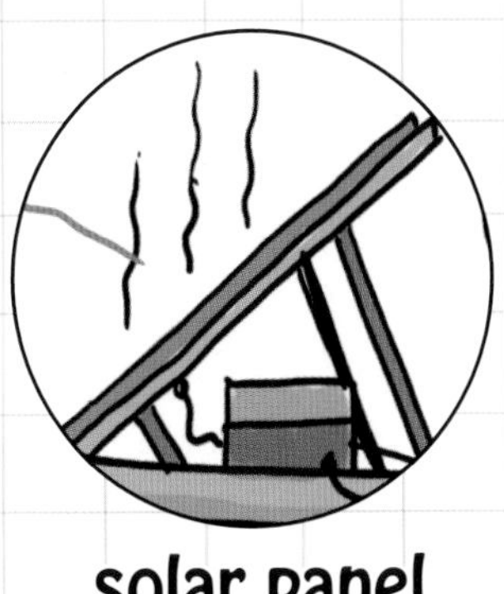
solar panel

Wind power comes from a small turbine next to the solar panels. The propeller turns when the wind blows against its blades. The power made by the turning blades is turned into electricity by a machine called a generator.

wind turbine

Rainwater is collected in tanks and used for washing and showering. It is also filtered and cleaned so it's safe to drink.

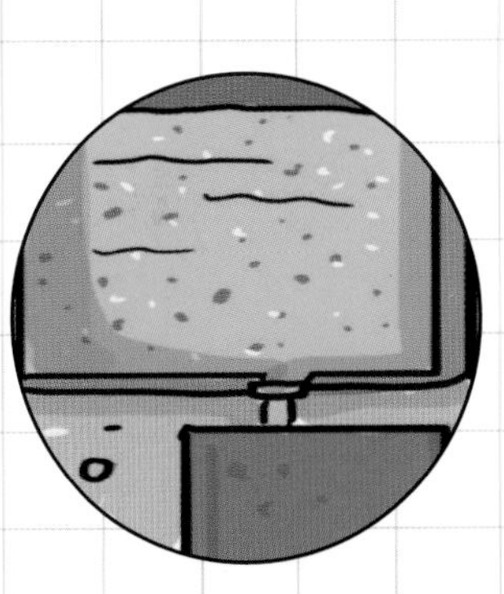
water tank

The windows that face south act like a greenhouse. This means that plants can survive inside the home all year round. People can grow their own vegetables both inside and outside.

plants

Recycled materials

Earthships are made of a lot of interesting materials, and some of them are things we normally throw away.

WHAT A WASTE!

More than 250 million used tires are scrapped each year in the United States.

In Japan, about 441,000 tons (400,000 metric tons) of bottles are recycled yearly.

In 2009, Brazil collected more than 40 million aluminum drink cans for recycling EVERY DAY!

Old tires are used to build thick walls. They are stacked just like bricks and can hold a lot of weight. They are also **fire resistant**, which means they don't burn easily. Once they are stacked, the tires are filled with soil, which is packed tightly until it is solid and even.

This is known as the rammed-earth technique. It is a method used all around the world.

Tires can also be made into roof tiles.

Natural wood and even whole trees can be recycled and used inside your home.

Plastic bottles can also be filled with a variety of materials, such as **adobe** or dirt, and used like bricks to make walls.

Bottles and cans are used to decorate the walls of this earthship.

Bottles and tin cans are other things you find in the recycling center. They are also a cheap alternative to bricks and can be reused to create attractive designs in the walls.

Green roof

A green roof is an amazing sight, but it isn't just for show. The plants growing on it help insulate the building. **Insulation** protects your house from changing temperatures, which means it stays warm in the winter and cool in the summer.

Traditional green roof houses in Icelan

A living roof, as it is often called, attracts wildlife to your home.

A green wall with growing plants and flowers

Green walls

Buildings in the city soak up sunlight and store the heat, which make the inside of the building hot. This is a problem in the summer when people want to stay cool.

Some modern architects plant gardens on the walls of buildings. Why? It's because the plants give off water vapor, a type of gas, which cools the air around them. They also provide shade and even insulate against the sound of the noisy traffic in the street below.

Solar home

The building on the opposite page has solar panels on the roof that collect sunlight to make electricity. They can rotate to follow the Sun. But that's not all! The entire **structure** can also rotate. To stay cool in the summer, it can turn away from the Sun. For warmth in the winter, it can face the Sun.

Solar houses make their own power, heat, and electricity. This is done with solar panels that use the Sun's energy.

On the Heliotrope building, panels on the roof turn to follow the Sun all the time. Because of this, the house makes more power than it uses. Not only that—all the balcony railings are filled with water, which is warmed by the Sun for showers and heat all over the building. Rainwater is also collected on the roof and waste water is filtered to use again!

SUMMER

WINTER

he Heliotrope
n Freiburg,
Germany

Drawing a plan

The Heliotrope house has three floors and a roof patio.

Every area of the building has a very specific purpose.

All electrical equipment is powered by the solar energy formed on the roof.

Second floor

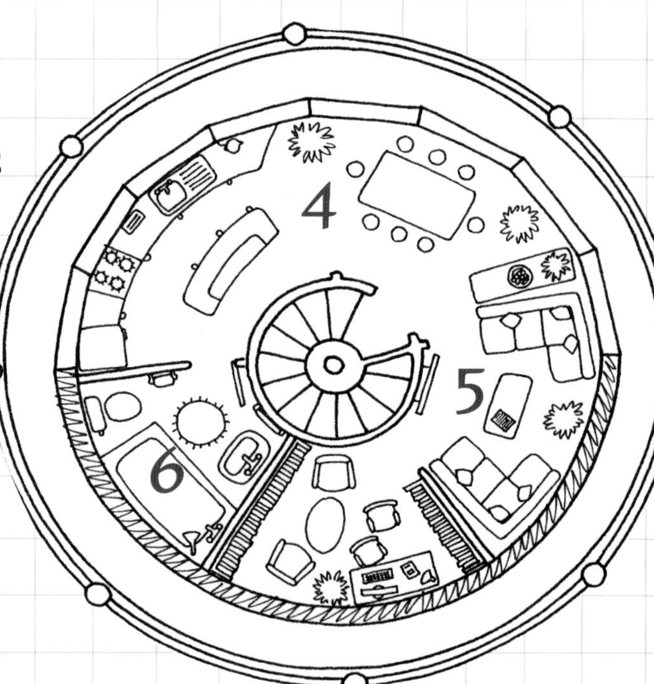

First floor

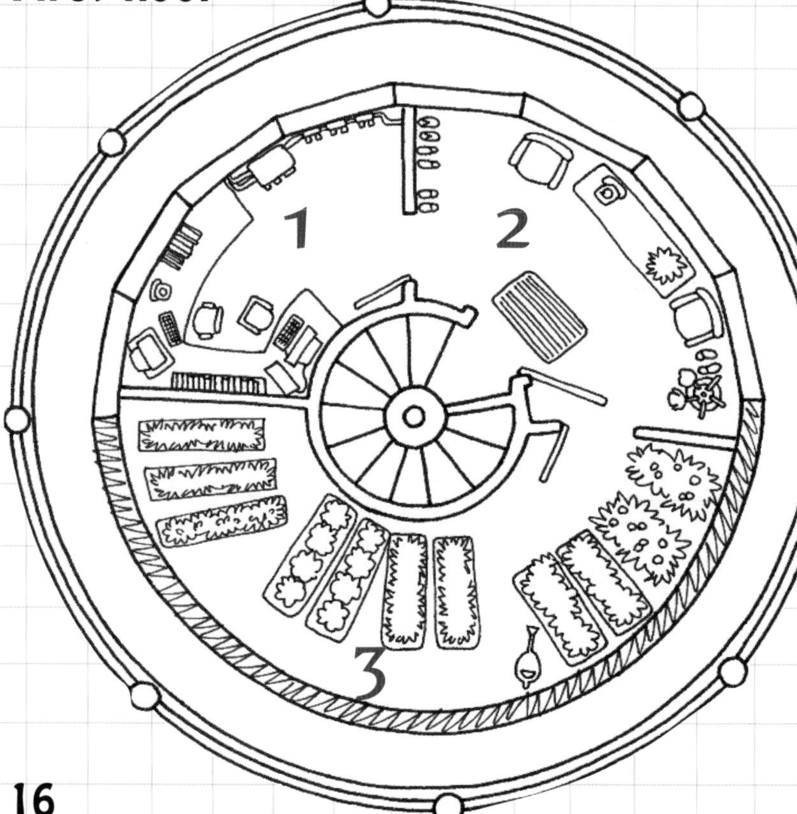

1. Control room
2. Workshop
3. Greenhouse
4. Kitchen
5. Living room
6. Bathroom

- Architect's words -

Floor plan

As soon as the client, or the person who wants the home built, explains what they want and need in their new home, the architect will draw a **floor plan**. This is a simple drawing which shows how the rooms and spaces in the building are organized and arranged.

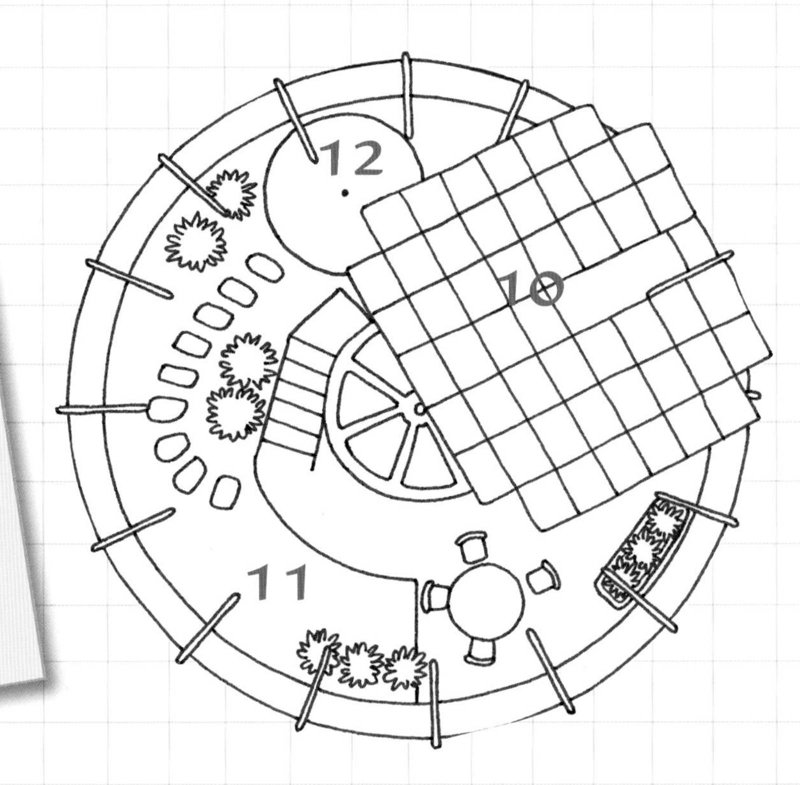

Roof

Third floor

7. Main bedroom
8. Solar heated railings
9. Playroom
10. Big solar panels
11. Patio garden
12. Water tank

Robinson Crusoe

Robinson Crusoe is a famous story written by Daniel Defoe nearly 300 years ago. It is about a sailor who gets **shipwrecked** on a tropical island and has to survive there for 28 years!

He learned many skills to stay alive. He built a home that provided him with shelter and a place to sleep.

He hunted fish and other animals for food.

He grew crops such as barley, rice, wild turnips, and cabbages.

He also kept goats for milk to make cheese

But **cannibals** were also living on the island! Crusoe managed to rescue one of their prisoners and called him Friday because that was the day they met. Together, they fought the cannibals. Then a ship arrived to save them and they could return home to England.

Build your own shelter

Just like Crusoe, you can build your own shelter using wood, **bamboo**, leafy branches, and grass.

1. You will need some long poles, which can be wood or bamboo.
2. Hammer them into the ground firmly. Place them in two lines at an angle, so they touch each other at the top. These are the wall supports.
3. Join them along the top with some more bamboo poles. Tie all the poles together with string. This makes the roof structure.
4. Cover the whole frame with leafy branches and grass.

Living off the land

- Architect's words -
Sustainable
Sustainable describes a way of living that helps the environment. It means you work hard to make sure you don't use too much power, such as electricity and heat. You also try to create your own power to replace what you use.

More and more people are trying to live more naturally. Just like Robinson Crusoe, people are growing their own vegetables and keeping animals, or livestock, to produce their own food.

By doing this, they don't need to use their cars to go shopping. Car engines burn fuels that are harmful to the environment. This way of life is called **self-sufficiency** and is a type of sustainable living.

Sustainable materials

People who live sustainably also live in **sustainable** homes. That means the materials used to build their houses are easily found in nature from the land around them. These materials will grow back over time.

Wood from sustainable forests means every tree that is cut down is replaced by a new one. This wood has a certificate to prove that it is sustainable.

:oconut trees, used for flooring
ınd wall tiles, will reach full height
ı only five years.

3amboo grows really fast
;o it is replaced quickly.

Adobe bricks are usually made with soil from the building site. This makes the material easy to find and provides another way to recycle.

Made of mud

Mud is a traditional building material that is **eco-friendly** because it uses soil and dirt taken from the site where the house is being built. This is great because it is natural, it doesn't need any transportation, and it's really cheap to produce. Mud buildings are found all over the world.

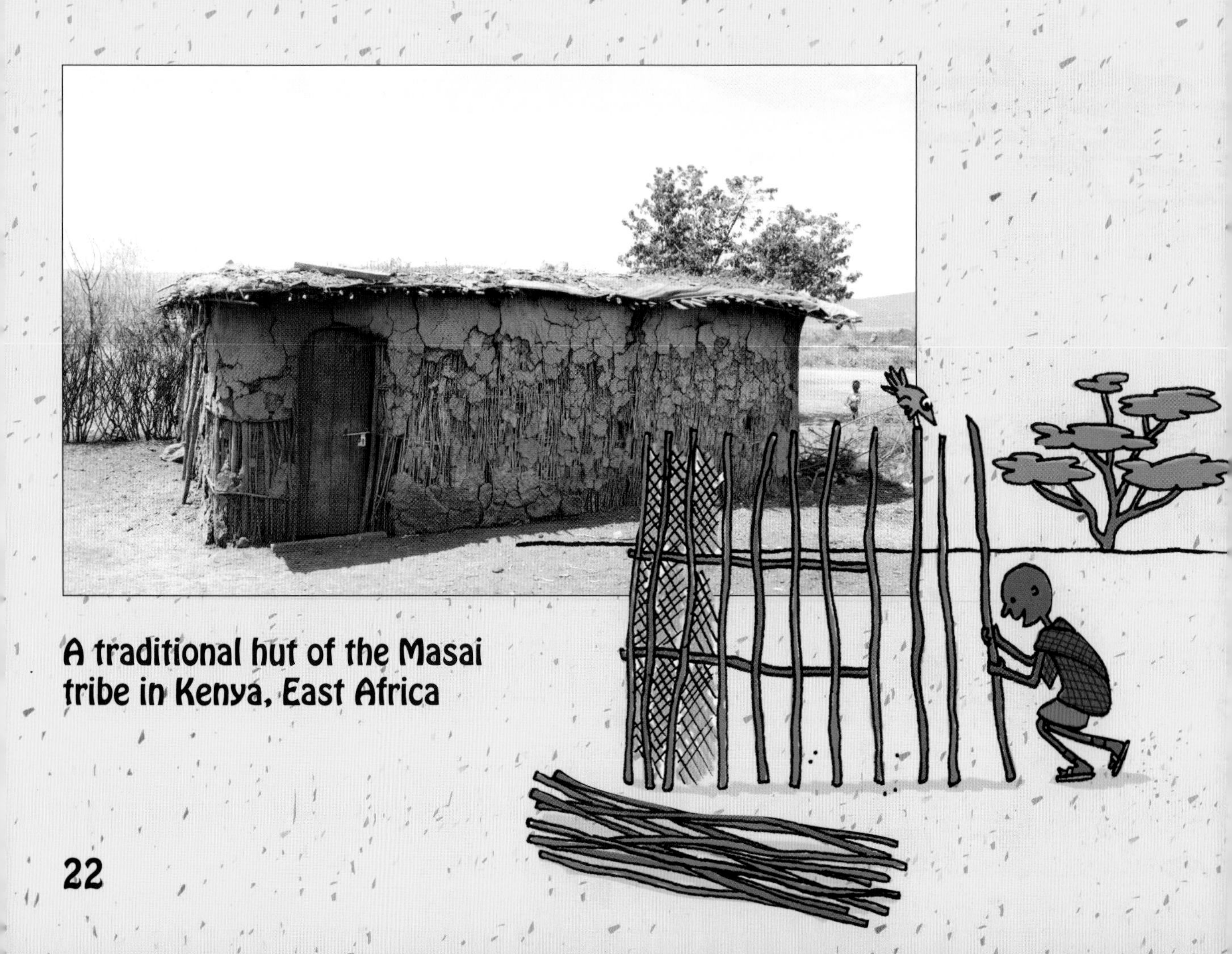

A traditional hut of the Masai tribe in Kenya, East Africa

A Native American house of the Navajo people in the U.S.

Mud is being used more and more in modern structures. Today, it is called adobe or **cob** construction.

A cob home in the U.S.

Cob and adobe use a mixture of mud, sand, clay, water, and straw to make cheap and colorful buildings of all shapes and sizes. Not only that, they are fire resistant and well-insulated!

A modern adobe home in New Mexico

Architect's notebook

Insulation

Insulation is very important in a green home. It prevents the house from getting too cold or hot, keeping it at a constant temperature all year round.

This means in winter, you don't need to heat your home as much and won't use as much fuel. In the summer, you don't need air conditioning, which uses a lot of electricity. Using too much electrical power or fuel is harmful to the environment, so insulation helps protect the house AND the planet.

The best insulation is made of natural materials such as wood fiber, sheep's wool, or cotton.

This house uses straw bales for walls.

One of the most unusual materials used for insulation is recycled paper that is sprayed on!

Bales of straw or logs, called **cordwood**, are also useful materials to use in your eco-home. They create thick walls that help insulate the house.

A look inside

The inside design of a green home is also the job of the architect, because furniture and features are built into the walls and floors.

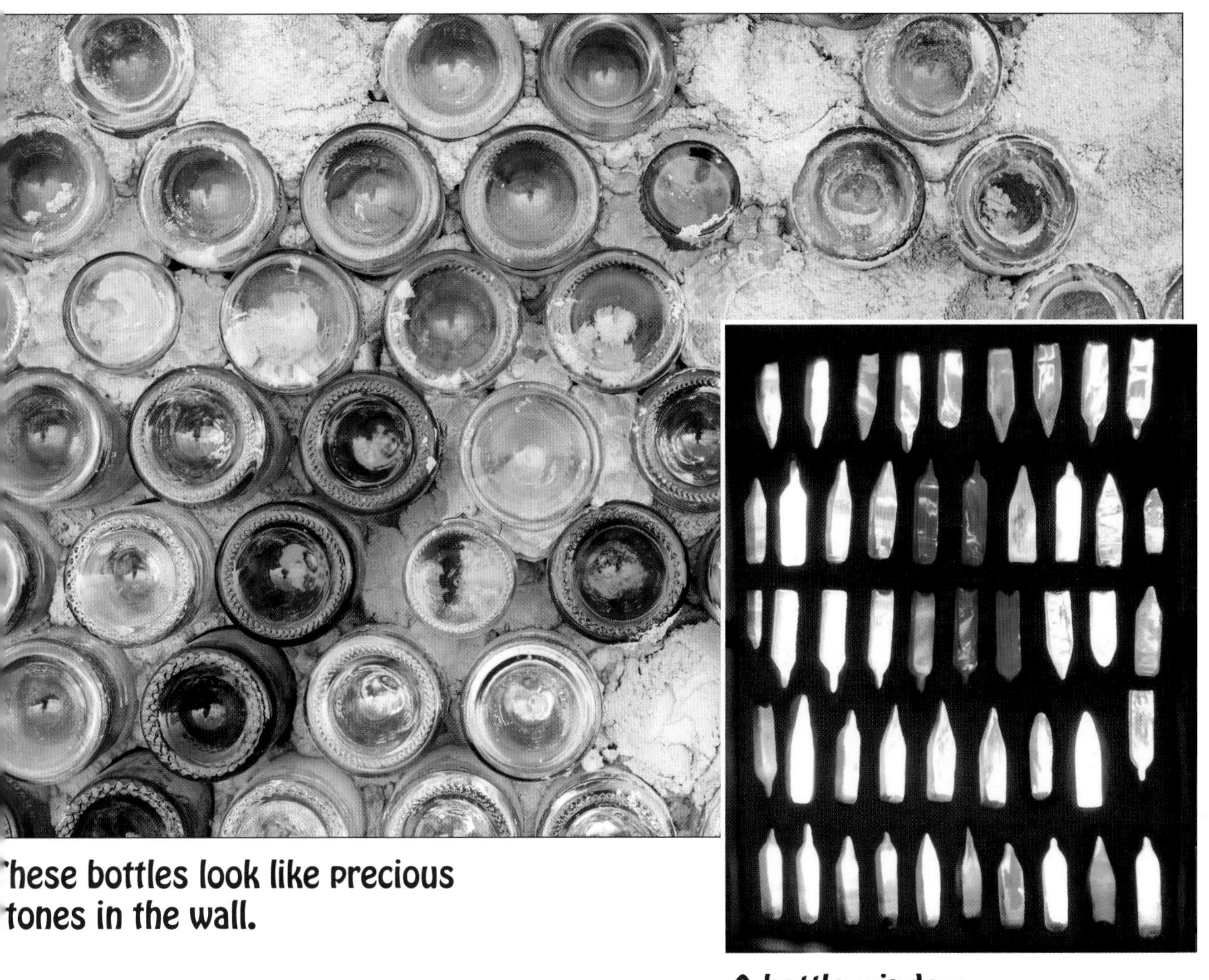

'hese bottles look like precious
'tones in the wall.

A bottle window

Beautiful bottles

Bottles can make really pretty patterns in an eco-home. By cutting the tops off the bottles and joining the bottom ends, the bottles can be used like bricks to make a wall. They are attached with mortar, a kind of bricklayer's glue made from limestone, cement, sand, and water.

Eco-communities

Today, architects are also designing whole communities, and even cities, which use green methods of building.

Chengdu Great City, China, is a city with thousands of people and designed so nobody needs a car.

Findhorn eco-village in Scotland is a community of people all living in green homes.

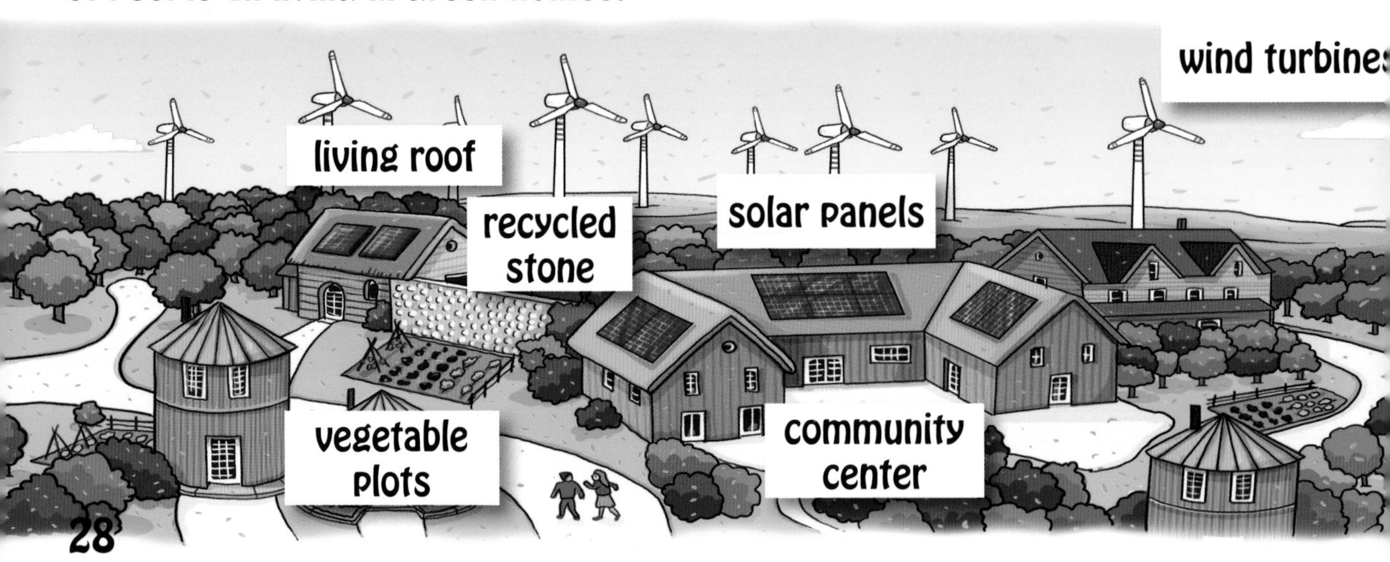

'he purpose of these designs is to create
:ommunities that use very little fuel or
naterials that are harmful to the environment.
'hey also create their own power and use
ustainable materials.

Glossary

adobe A building material made of sand, mud, and straw

bamboo A tall tropical grass used for building and furniture making

cannibal A human being who eats people

cob A building material made of mud, sand, clay, water, and straw

cordwood A building style that uses short lengths of wood instead of bricks

eco-friendly A description of something that is natural or not harmful to the environment

external The outside part of something

fire resistant Something that doesn't burn easily

floor plan An outline drawing that shows the layout of a building

insulation Materials placed in or on a building's walls to protect the inside of the building from changing temperatures

internal The inside of something

photovoltaic cell A specially treated plate that changes sunlight into electricity

self-sufficiency A style of life where people grow their own food and create their own power

septic tank A tank that holds human waste

shipwrecked When a sailor experiences a loss or destruction of their ship

solar panels A group of photovoltaic cells arranged on a flat board in order to convert sunlight to electricity

structure Another name for the framework of a building

sustainable A resource that is easily grown or created that doesn't overuse or reduce the natural supply

wind turbine A type of turning blade which uses the power of wind to create electricity

Learning more

ooks:

ridgewater, Alan and Gill Bridgewater.
co Kids Self-Sufficiency Handbook.
hatswood, Australia: New Holland, 2009.
his guide features ideas from green projects
hat lead readers to a more green and
ustainable life.

arthWorks Group and Sophie Javna.
*he New 50 Simple Things Kids Can Do
o Save the Earth.* Kansas City, MO:
ndrews McMeel Publishing, 2009.
his book gives projects, links, and tips
hat young readers can use to help preserve
ur Earth.

wlkids Magazine. *Try This at Home: Planet-
riendly Projects for Kids.* Ontario, Canada:
wlkids Books, 2009.
his book gives young eco-activists
o-it-yourself projects and information
or ways they can live green.

Websites:

http://shrinkthatfootprint.com/beyond-efficiency-sustainable-home
This article gives the five most important considerations when building a green home.

www.eia.gov/kids/energy.cfm?page=solar_home-basics
Energy kids provides information about solar energy and how it works.

www.eia.gov/kids/energy.cfm?page=wind_home-basics
Energy kids explains wind and how its power is harnessed to make electricity.

www.childrenoftheearth.org/green-building-sustainable-homes/green-homes-sustainable-living-index.htm
Simple tips with explanations show readers the ways home-building can be made greener and more sustainable.

http://pbskids.org/eekoworld/
This site gives information about the environment and a variety of ways children can help protect it.

Index